My Godfather A to Z

Fill In The Blank Gift Book

Printed in USA

Published by K. Francklin

Cover Image: Produced by K. Francklin

© Copyright 2015

ISBN-13: 978-1519788504

ISBN-10: 1519788509

I'm Glad You're My Godfather Because...

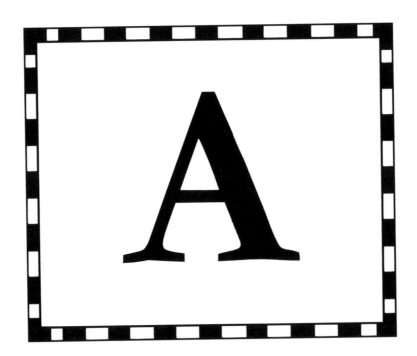

You are...

A_____

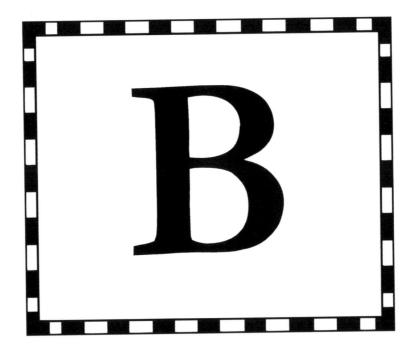

You are...

B_____

You are...

C<u>   </u>

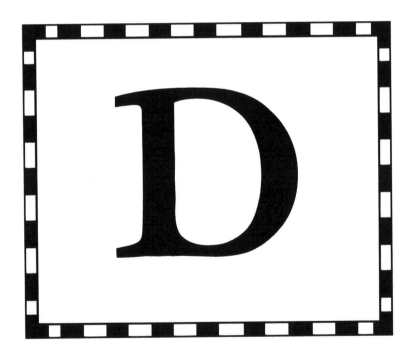

You are...

D_____

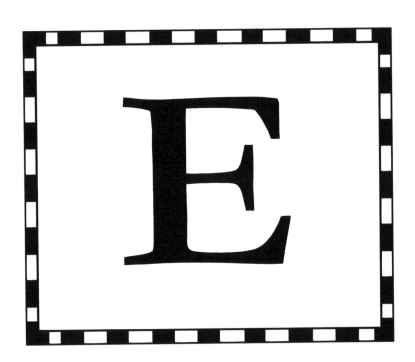

You are...

E_____

You are...

F_____

You are...

G_____

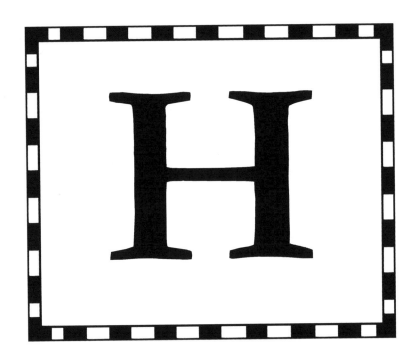

You are…

H_____

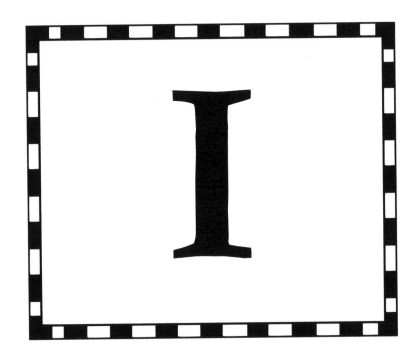

You are...

I_____

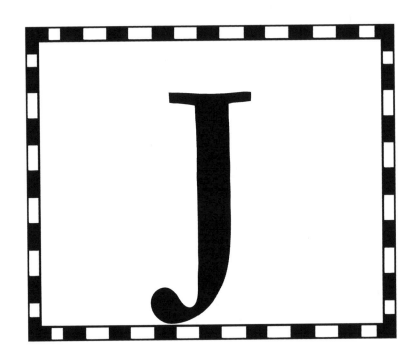

You are...

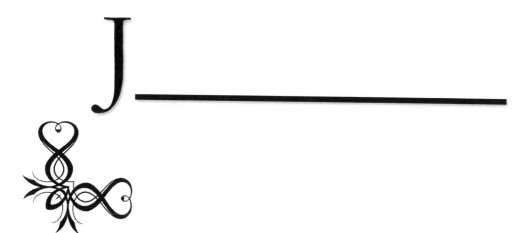

J_____

You are...

K_____

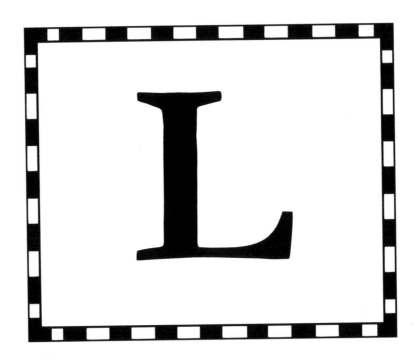

You are...

L_____

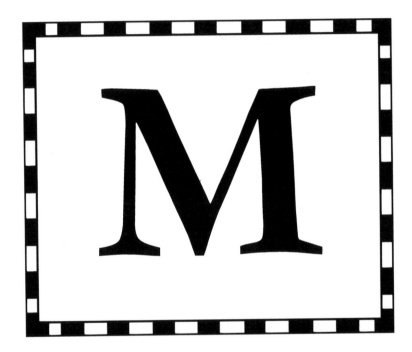

You are...

M_____

You are...

N_____

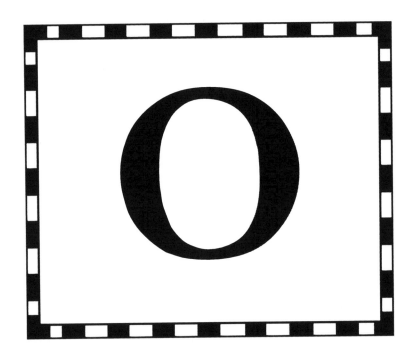

You are...

O_____

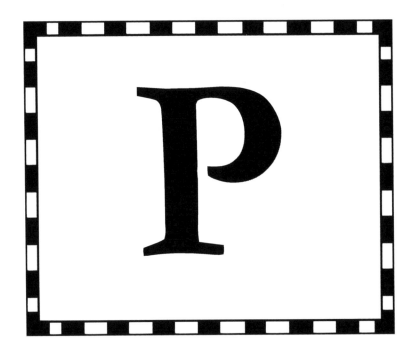

You are...

P_____

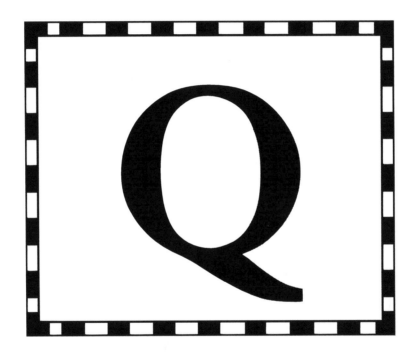

You are...

Q_____

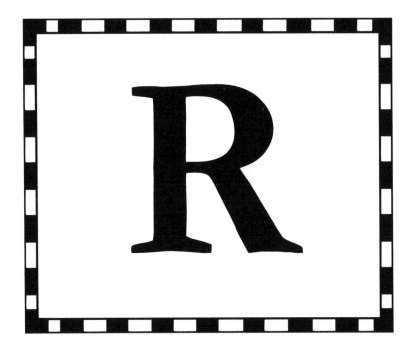

You are...

R_____

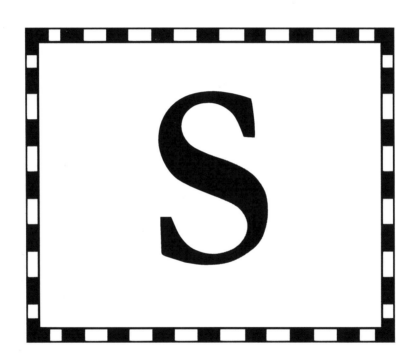

You are...

S_____

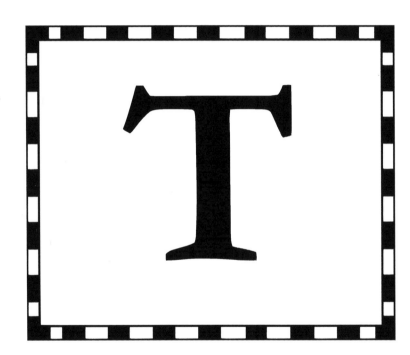

You are...

T_____

You are…

U_____

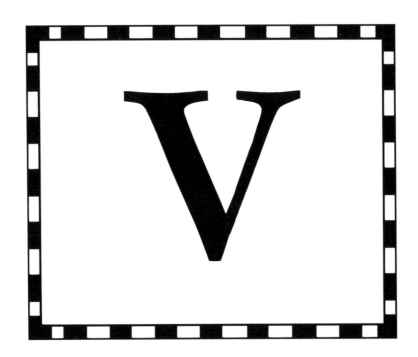

You are...

V_____

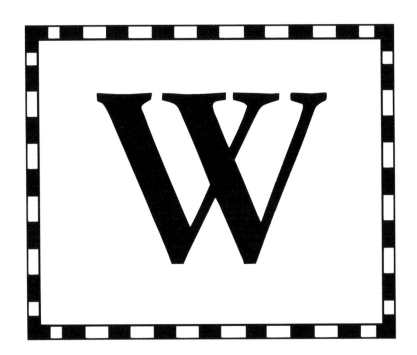

You are...

W_____

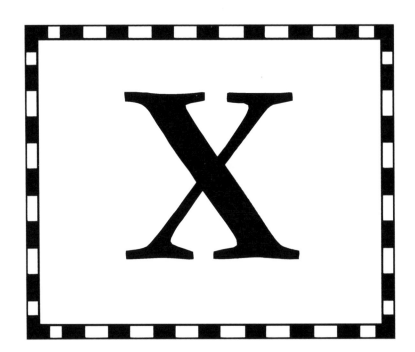

You are…

X_____

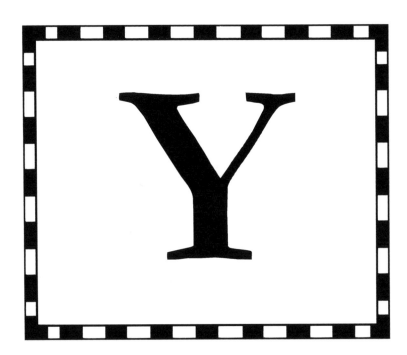

You are...

Y_____

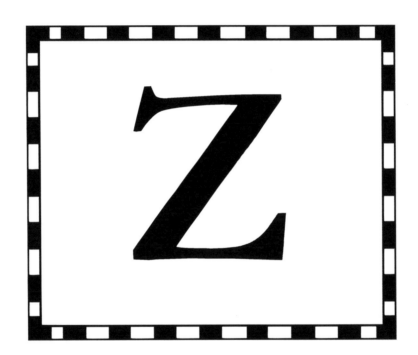

You are...

Z_____

Thank You!

Also In This Series

My Dad/Papa/Step Dad A to Z

My Mom/Mum/Mama/Step Mom/Mum A to Z

My Son/Daughter A to Z

My Husband/Wife A to Z

My Brother (Little, Older)/Sister (Little, Older)/Twin A to Z

My Uncle/Aunt/Auntie/Aunty A to Z

My Grandpa/Grandad/Gramps/Grampy A to Z

My Grandma/Granny/Nanny/Gran/Nana/Nan A to Z

My Best Friend/Bestie/Someone Special/Roommate A to Z

My Girlfriend/Boyfriend/Lover A to Z

My Partner/Valentine/ Fiancée/Fiancé A to Z

My Cousin/Nephew/Niece A to Z

My Teacher/Boss/Hairdresser/Pastor A to Z

My Bridesmaid A to Z

My In Laws (Father/Mother/Brother/Sister/Daughter/Son)

My Godmother/Godfather

Made in the USA
Middletown, DE
14 December 2017